Wonderful
Words of Life

© 2012 by Barbour Publishing, Inc.

Written and compiled by Joanna Bloss.

Print ISBN 978-1-62029-184-9

eBook Editions:
Adobe Digital Edition (.epub) 978-1-62029-650-9
Kindle and MobiPocket Edition (.prc) 978-1-62029-649-3

Published by Barbour Publishing, Inc., P.O. Box 719, Uhrichsville, Ohio 44683, www.barbourbooks.com

Our mission is to publish and distribute inspirational products offering exceptional value and biblical encouragement to the masses.

 Member of the Evangelical Christian Publishers Association

Printed in the United States of America.

Wonderful
Words of Life

Inspiration from the Beloved Hymn

BARBOUR
PUBLISHING

CONTENTS

Wonderful Words of Life

Sing them over again to me,
Wonderful words of life,
Let me more of their beauty see,
Wonderful words of life;
Words of life and beauty
Teach me faith and duty.

Chorus:
Beautiful words, wonderful words,
Wonderful words of life;
Beautiful words, wonderful words,
Wonderful words of life.

Christ, the blessed One, gives to all
Wonderful words of life;
Sinner, listen to the loving call,
Wonderful words of life;
All so freely given,
Wooing us to heaven.

Sweetly echo the Gospel call,
Wonderful words of life;
Offer pardon and peace to all,
Wonderful words of life;
Jesus, only Savior,
Sanctify us forever.

PHILIP P. BLISS, 1874

Words of Life

In the beginning was the Word,
and the Word was with God,
and the Word was God. . . .
In Him was life,
and the life was the Light of men.

JOHN 1:1, 4 NASB

$\mathcal{E}$very day, Jesus encountered people who were oppressed, poor, and without hope. They were harassed and helpless, sheep without a shepherd (Matthew 9:36). Each word spoken by the Word offered life to their dry and weary souls. While He warned that Satan would try to kill, steal, and destroy that hope, He promised a rich and abundant life to all who would confess and believe on His name.

As promising as they were then and are today, Jesus' words are also ironic, because abundant life typically doesn't mean our circumstances will change. He doesn't always remove the hardship, the storms, the pain, or the oppression. He does, however, allow us to experience inexplicable peace in the midst of the storm, hope in the midst of pain, and mighty strength in the midst of helplessness.

In the pages that follow are Jesus' wonderful words of Life. Embrace them for all the life they have to offer you.

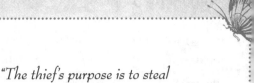

"The thief's purpose is to steal
and kill and destroy.
My purpose is to give them
a rich and satisfying life."

JOHN 10:10 NLT

For those who find me [wisdom] find life
and receive favor from the LORD.

PROVERBS 8:35 NIV

Now all glory to God, who is able, through his
mighty power at work within us, to accomplish
infinitely more than we might ask or think.

EPHESIANS 3:20 NLT

Three keys to more abundant living:
caring about others,
daring for others,
sharing with others.
WILLIAM ARTHUR WARD

Not only do we know God by
Jesus Christ alone, but we know
ourselves only by Jesus Christ.
Apart from Jesus Christ, we do not
know what is our life, nor our death,
nor God, nor ourselves.
BLAISE PASCAL

O LORD, I give my life to you.

PSALM 25:1 NLT

*"For life is more than food,
and your body more than clothing."*

LUKE 12:23 NLT

*This means that anyone who
belongs to Christ has become a new person.
The old life is gone; a new life has begun!*

2 CORINTHIANS 5:17 NLT

A Prayer for Life

Father, I am amazed that no detail of my life is too small for You. I am thankful that You offer abundant life through Jesus. Thank You for this gift. Expand my awareness of what it means to live a rich and satisfying life, and may I always do so, to the glory of Your name. Amen.

For you died to this life,
and your real life is hidden
with Christ in God.

COLOSSIANS 3:3 NLT

"The Spirit gives life;
the flesh counts for nothing.
The words I have spoken to you—
they are full of the Spirit and life."

JOHN 6:63 NIV

My life is an example to many,
because you have been
my strength and protection.

PSALM 71:7 NLT

When I no more can stir my soul to move,
And life is but the ashes of a fire;
When I can but remember that my heart
Once used to live and love, long and aspire—
O be thou then the first, the one thou art;
Be thou the calling, before all answering love,
And in me wake hope, fear, boundless desire.

GEORGE MACDONALD

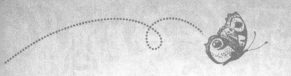

"I am the bread of life.
Whoever comes to me will
never go hungry, and whoever
believes in me will never be thirsty."

JOHN 6:35 NIV

Listen carefully to my words.
Don't lose sight of them.
Let them penetrate deep into your heart,
for they bring life to those who find them,
and healing to their whole body.

PROVERBS 4:20–22 NLT

Capture My Attention

Jesus, I confess that I am distracted
by many things that interfere
with my ability to live abundantly for You.
I pray that You would free me
from the temptation to lose myself
in trivial matters. Instead, capture my
attention and draw it to You,
and You alone. Amen.

Our days are numbered. One of the primary goals in our lives should be to prepare for our last day. The legacy we leave is not just in our possessions, but in the quality of our lives. What preparations should we be making now? The greatest waste in all of our earth, which cannot be recycled or reclaimed, is our waste of the time that God has given us each day.

BILLY GRAHAM

Words of Truth

"*I am. . .the truth.*"

JOHN 14:6 NIV

The rich young ruler was wealthy. He didn't lie, cheat, or steal. He hadn't killed anyone. He honored his parents, was kind to his neighbors. He was still missing something, and he knew Jesus would have the answer. "What good thing must I do to get eternal life?" he asked (Matthew 19:16 NIV). In His usual, no-nonsense fashion, Jesus delivered the truth: "If you want to be perfect, go, sell your possessions and give to the poor, and you will have treasure in heaven. Then come, follow me." This was a hard truth to swallow, especially for a rich man. He walked away. Others, like the disciples, dropped everything to follow Him. Some wept at His feet, others knew if they merely touched the hem of His garment, they would be forever changed.

Whether they were rich or poor, powerful or despised, everyone Jesus encountered had no choice but to respond to His truth. There was no middle ground. They either received it and acted on it, or rejected it and walked away.

You have this same opportunity. How will you respond to His truth?

"So if the Son sets you free, you are truly free."

JOHN 8:36 NLT

Guide me in your truth and teach me,
for you are God my Savior,
and my hope is in you all day long.

PSALM 25:5 NIV

Β

They exchanged the truth about God for a lie,
and worshiped and served created things rather
than the Creator—who is forever praised. Amen.

ROMANS 1:25 NIV

Half a truth is often a great lie.

BENJAMIN FRANKLIN

He that takes truth for his guide,
and duty for his end, may safely trust
God's providence to lead him aright.

BLAISE PASCAL

Whoever is careless with the
truth in small matters cannot
be trusted with important matters.

ALBERT EINSTEIN

Love does not delight in evil
but rejoices with the truth.

1 CORINTHIANS 13:6 NIV

"If you hold to my teaching, you are really
my disciples. Then you will know the truth,
and the truth will set you free."

JOHN 8:31–32 NIV

Dear children, let us not love with words
or speech but with actions and in truth.

1 JOHN 3:18 NIV

A Prayer for Truth

Jesus, thank You for Your message
of truth. I want to respond in
faithfulness and obedience. I long
to grow in my understanding of
Your truth, allow it to permeate
my life. Guide me in Your truth
and teach me, all day long. Amen.

*And do not take the word of
truth utterly out of my mouth,
for I wait for your ordinances.*
PSALM 119:43 NASB

*"My mouth speaks what is true,
for my lips detest wickedness."*
PROVERBS 8:7 NIV

*He will wear righteousness like a
belt and truth like an undergarment.*
ISAIAH 11:5 NLT

Thou art the bread of life, O Lord, to me,
Thy holy Word the truth that saveth me;
Give me to eat and live with Thee above;
Teach me to love Thy truth, for Thou art love.

MARY A. LATHBURY

Peace, if possible, truth at all costs.

MARTIN LUTHER

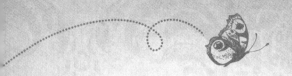

*No one who practices deceit will
dwell in my house; no one who speaks
falsely will stand in my presence.*

PSALM 101:7 NIV

*Get the truth and never sell it; also get wisdom,
discipline, and good judgment.*

PROVERBS 23:23 NLT

*Truthful lips endure forever,
but a lying tongue lasts only a moment.*

PROVERBS 12:19 NIV

Prayer for an Honest Heart

Father, one of the greatest barriers to truth is my inability to be honest with myself. I struggle to acknowledge my faults and imperfections, and instead I rationalize and justify in an effort to make myself seem better than I am. Help me to be honest with You about my shortcomings. Thank You for patiently guiding me closer and closer to the truth. Amen.

I believe that in the end,
truth will conquer.

JOHN WYCLIFFE

God's truth judges created things
out of love, and Satan's truth judges
them out of envy and hatred.

DIETRICH BONHOEFFER

Words of Beauty

Jesus replied, "Leave her alone.
She did this in preparation for my burial.
You will always have the poor among you,
but you will not always have me."

JOHN 12:7–8 NLT

Perhaps Mary had been saving the jar of expensive perfume for a special occasion, maybe the wedding of a friend or a family celebration. But this night, as she prepared to dine with Jesus and His disciples, she knew the moment had arrived. In a simple act of beauty, she lovingly anointed Jesus' feet and wiped them with her hair.

Is it possible she knew what was to come? Did she know His feet would soon walk the long road to Calvary, or that in a very short time, nails would pierce His precious flesh? Perhaps, but perhaps she was merely overwhelmed by love for her beloved friend, the one who wept when she wept. Not quite the stuff of beauty, washing feet, but devotion to her Lord made it all worthwhile. Judas, his eyes blinded by sin and ulterior motive, was incapable of seeing the beauty in this quiet moment. He missed it entirely. Only those of a pure heart and mind can see the beauty of the Lord.

*Charm is deceptive, and beauty
does not last; but a woman who fears
the LORD will be greatly praised.*
PROVERBS 31:30 NLT

*"How beautiful are the feet of
those who bring good news!"*
ROMANS 10:15 NIV

Since love grows within you, so beauty grows.
For love is the beauty of the soul.
SAINT AUGUSTINE

Never say there is nothing beautiful in
the world anymore. There is always
something to make you wonder in the
shape of a tree, the trembling of a leaf.
ALBERT SCHWEITZER

The greatest treasures are those invisible
to the eye but found by the heart.
UNKNOWN

*So God created human beings in
his own image. In the image
of God he created them.*

GENESIS 1:27 NLT

*Don't be concerned about the outward
beauty of fancy hairstyles, expensive jewelry,
or beautiful clothes. You should clothe yourselves
instead with the beauty that comes from within,
the unfading beauty of a gentle and quiet spirit,
which is so precious to God.*

1 PETER 3:3–4 NLT

I Long to See Your Beauty

Lord Jesus, Your beauty surrounds me,
but sometimes I miss it. Open my heart and
my eyes so that I might gaze on Your beauty,
and soak it in to the depths of my soul. Fill me
with love and adoration for You, and help me
to find ways to honor You through simple acts
of beauty and grace. Amen.

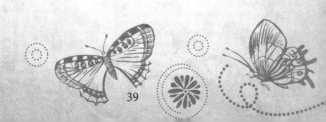

Let the king be enthralled by your beauty;
honor him, for he is your lord.

PSALM 45:11 NIV

One thing I ask from the LORD,
this only do I seek: that I may dwell
in the house of the LORD all the days
of my life, to gaze on the beauty of the
LORD and to seek him in his temple.

PSALM 27:4 NIV

The most beautiful things in the world
cannot be seen or even touched;
they must be felt with the heart.

HELEN KELLER

Beauty is the gift of God.

ARISTOTLE

Worship the Lord in the beauty of holiness,
Bow down before Him, His glory proclaim;
Gold of obedience and incense of lowliness,
Bring and adore Him—the Lord is His Name.

JOHN S. B. MONSELL

He will give a crown of beauty for ashes,
a joyous blessing instead of mourning,
festive praise instead of despair. In their
righteousness, they will be like great oaks that
the LORD has planted for his own glory.

ISAIAH 61:3 NLT

How beautiful you are, my darling,
how beautiful! Your eyes are like doves.

SONG OF SOLOMON 1:15 NLT

A Gentle and Quiet Spirit

Father, in a world filled with
visual images and man-made
trinkets, it is easy to lose sight
of what true beauty is. Instead of
investing my time and money in
cultivating my outward beauty,
which does not last, help me to
pour my resources into cultivating
a gentle and quiet spirit,
the qualities you desire in a
woman who loves You. Amen.

My life is but a weaving
Between my God and me.
I cannot choose the colors
He weaveth steadily.
Oft' times He weaveth sorrow;
And I in foolish pride
Forget He sees the upper
And I the underside.
Not till the loom is silent
And the shuttles cease to fly
Will God unroll the canvas
And reveal the reason why.

CORRIE TEN BOOM

Words of Faith

*Jesus turned around, and when he saw
her he said, "Daughter, be encouraged!
Your faith has made you well."*

MATTHEW 9:22 NLT

She had exhausted her resources. She visited doctor after doctor, desperate for a cure, as the life drained out of her, her health worsening by the day. Then she heard about Jesus, a man they called the Healer. Somehow she knew if she could just touch Him—ever so briefly—she would be made well. When her childlike faith encountered the mighty touch of the Healer, the charge was electric. He felt the power leave Him and touch her to the core. Her life would never be the same. She was free.

Did this woman consider herself to possess great faith? Doubtful. It seems she reached out to Him more out of desperation than mountain-moving faith. However, Jesus promised that a mustard-seed speck is all that's required. Do you have even a mustard seed's worth of faith? Reach out with it, and touch Him. You will never be the same.

*"I do believe; help me
overcome my unbelief!"*
MARK 9:24 NIV

*He replied, "You of little faith, why are you so
afraid?" Then he got up and rebuked the winds
and the waves, and it was completely calm.*
MATTHEW 8:26 NIV

*And Abram believed the LORD, and the LORD
counted him as righteous because of his faith.*
GENESIS 15:6 NLT

The whole being of any Christian is faith
and love. Faith brings the man to God,
love brings him to men.

MARTIN LUTHER

Faith, mighty faith, the promise sees,
and looks to God alone; laughs at
impossibilities, and cries it shall be done.

CHARLES WESLEY

Fight the good fight for the true faith.
Hold tightly to the eternal life to which
God has called you, which you have
confessed so well before many witnesses.

1 TIMOTHY 6:12 NLT

Faith is the confidence that what we
hope for will actually happen; it gives
us assurance about things we cannot see.

HEBREWS 11:1 NLT

Increase My Faith

Father, as I read through scripture,
it is impossible not to be amazed
by Your miracles, by the stories
of lives changed, promises kept,
and hope made alive.
But I confess that my faith wavers
when I become mired in the
circumstances of my own life,
when I start to look around, and
not up. I pray that You would keep
my eyes laser focused on You,
and increase my faith. Amen.

I will sing of the LORD's great love forever;
with my mouth I will make your faithfulness
known through all generations.

PSALM 89:1 NIV

"Truly I tell you, if you have faith as small
as a mustard seed, you can say to this
mountain, 'Move from here to there,' and it will
move. Nothing will be impossible for you."

MATTHEW 17:20 NIV

Faith is to believe what you do not see;
the reward of this faith is to see what you believe.

SAINT AUGUSTINE

I have found there are three stages to every
great work of God: first it is impossible,
then it is difficult, then it is done.

J. HUDSON TAYLOR

Faith is what makes life bearable,
with all its tragedies and ambiguities
and sudden, startling joys.

MADELEINE L'ENGLE

For you know that when your faith is tested,
your endurance has a chance to grow.

JAMES 1:3 NLT

And it is impossible to please God without
faith. Anyone who wants to come to him
must believe that God exists and that he
rewards those who sincerely seek him.

HEBREWS 11:6 NLT

Just as the body is dead without breath,
so also faith is dead without good works.

JAMES 2:26 NLT

A Grateful Heart

Jesus, forgive me for the times when I have
tried to earn the gift of salvation by doing
things merely to capture Your attention, trying
to prove myself worthy of Your love. Help my
good works to flow out of a grateful heart,
not a performing heart. Amen.

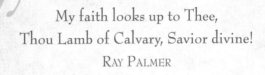

My faith looks up to Thee,
Thou Lamb of Calvary, Savior divine!

RAY PALMER

Be like the bird that, passing on her
flight awhile on boughs too slight,
feels them give way beneath her,
and yet sings, knowing that she hath wings.

VICTOR HUGO

Weave in faith and God
will find the thread.

UNKNOWN

Words of Duty

Jesus replied, "And you experts in the law, woe to you, because you load people down with burdens they can hardly carry, and you yourselves will not lift one finger to help them."

LUKE 11:46 NIV

While many of those who encountered Jesus were healed, freed, and transformed, the Pharisees were merely infuriated. Every word Jesus spoke cut straight to their hearts, but rather than allowing His truths to change them, they plotted to kill Him. Jesus and the Pharisees most often butted heads over the law. What was originally established to point the way to Christ had been reworked and adulterated, turned into a list of dos and don'ts that even the most righteous could never begin to uphold.

Although the Christian life is one of duty, Jesus challenged the Pharisees because they had "neglected the more important matters of the law—justice, mercy and faithfulness" (Matthew 23:23 NIV). They were so swallowed up in the details that the entire point had been long lost. Instead, Jesus asks that our duty flow out of grateful hearts that long to please Him.

The Lord says: "These people come near
to me with their mouth and honor me with
their lips, but their hearts are far from me.
Their worship of me is based on merely
human rules they have been taught."

ISAIAH 29:13 NIV

"Do not work for food that spoils, but for
food that endures to eternal life,
which the Son of Man will give you."

JOHN 6:27 NIV

Obedience is easy when you know
you are being guided by a God
who never makes mistakes.

CORRIE TEN BOOM

O how happy are they
Who the Savior obey,
And have laid up their treasure above!
Tongue cannot express
The sweet comfort and peace
Of a soul in its earliest love.

CHARLES WESLEY

Fear God and work hard.

DAVID LIVINGSTONE

The LORD has told you what is good, and this is what he requires of you: to do what is right, to love mercy, and to walk humbly with your God.

MICAH 6:8 NLT

But Samuel replied: "Does the LORD delight in burnt offerings and sacrifices as much as in obeying the LORD? To obey is better than sacrifice."

1 SAMUEL 15:22 NIV

The Spirit of the Law

Heavenly Father, thank You
for Your law. It teaches me and
instructs me; it shows me the
way I should go. I confess that
I sometimes get caught up in
the details, which makes me
judgmental of others and myself.
Help me to follow the spirit of
Your law and attend to its most
important elements—mercy,
justice, and faithfulness. Amen.

" 'You must obey my laws and
be careful to follow my decrees.
I am the LORD your God.' "

LEVITICUS 18:4 NIV

Do not add to or subtract from these
commands I am giving you. Just obey
the commands of the LORD your
God that I am giving you.

DEUTERONOMY 4:2 NLT

Do all the good you can, in all the ways you
can, to all the souls you can, in every place you
can, at all the times you can, with all the zeal
you can, as long as ever you can.

JOHN WESLEY

True holiness comes in doing
God's will with a smile.

MOTHER TERESA

Trust and obey, for there's no other way to
be happy in Jesus but to trust and obey.

JOHN SAMMIS

Jesus replied, "'You must love the LORD your God
with all your heart, all your soul, and all your mind.'
This is the first and greatest commandment.
A second is equally important: 'Love your neighbor
as yourself.' The entire law and all the demands of the
prophets are based on these two commandments."

MATTHEW 22:37–40 NLT

Teach My Heart to Love

Heavenly Father, loving You with all my heart,
soul, and mind is the essence of obedience.
Expand my love for You as I grow in my
understanding of Your great love for me.
Then I will be free to love others and live
a life that pleases You. Amen.

Let any man turn to God in earnest, let him begin to exercise himself unto godliness, let him seek to develop his powers of spiritual receptivity by trust and obedience and humility, and the results will exceed anything he may have hoped in his life.

A. W. TOZER

Words of Blessing

Then Jesus called for the children and said to the disciples, "Let the children come to me. Don't stop them! For the Kingdom of God belongs to those who are like these children."

LUKE 18:16 NLT

The Sunday school version is idyllic. The dewy faced children sit at Jesus' feet, quietly gazing up at Him, waiting to hear what He will say. In reality, they were probably running and playing, interrupting grown-up conversations with their runny noses and dirt-smudged knees. The disciples were annoyed by their presence, scolding the parents for having such unruly children.

Jesus saw them differently—interrupting their play for a moment, inviting them to come near. They skidded to a stop, surprised this gentle stranger might have something to say to them. And then He blessed them—gave them God's kingdom. The disciples must have been shocked that Jesus gave such a high place of honor to these bedraggled children.

Skid to a stop and turn to your Savior, right now, just as you are. He longs to lavish His blessing upon you.

"God blesses those who are humble, for they will inherit the whole earth. God blesses those who hunger and thirst for justice, for they will be satisfied. God blesses those who are merciful, for they will be shown mercy. God blesses those whose hearts are pure, for they will see God. God blesses those who work for peace, for they will be called the children of God."

MATTHEW 5:5–9 NLT

Just as I Am

Abba Father, Daddy. What a joy it is to be Your child. How freeing it is to know that I don't have to clean myself up to come before You. That You want me just as I am—not the scrubbed-up Sunday school version of me, but the Saturday-morning-playing-in-the-mud one who doesn't quite have it all together. May nothing hinder me from running straight into Your arms. Amen.

*From his abundance we have all received
one gracious blessing after another.*
JOHN 1:16 NLT

⊙

*LORD, you alone are my inheritance,
my cup of blessing. You guard all that is mine.*
PSALM 16:5 NLT

⊙

*The blessing of the LORD brings wealth,
without painful toil for it.*
PROVERBS 10:22 NIV

It is not how much we have, but how much we enjoy, that makes happiness.

CHARLES SPURGEON

Showers of blessing, showers of blessing we need. Mercy drops round us are falling, but for the showers we plead.

DANIEL H. WHITTLE

"For I will pour water on the thirsty land,
and streams on the dry ground;
I will pour out my Spirit on your offspring,
and my blessing on your descendants."

ISAIAH 44:3 NIV

" 'I will make them and the places surrounding my
hill a blessing. I will send down showers in season;
there will be showers of blessing.' "

EZEKIEL 34:26 NIV

Prayer for a Jealous Heart

Father, I confess that sometimes, when I see how
You have blessed others, my heart feels a little
jealous and perturbed. When I am in this state,
I am blinded to my own blessings. I forget that
my Father owns the cattle on a thousand hills,
that there is more than enough to go around.
Open my heart and my eyes to gratefully see and
receive my unique blessings. Amen.

"Bring all the tithes into the storehouse
so there will be enough food in my Temple.
If you do," says the LORD of Heaven's
Armies, "I will open the windows of heaven
for you. I will pour out a blessing so great
you won't have enough room to take it in!
Try it! Put me to the test!"

MALACHI 3:10 NLT

We failed, but in the good providence of God,
apparent failure often proves a blessing.

ROBERT E. LEE

May God give you. . .for every storm a
rainbow, for every tear a smile, for every
care a promise, and a blessing in each trial.
For every problem life sends, a faithful
friend to share, for every sigh a sweet song,
and an answer for each prayer.

IRISH BLESSING

Praise be to the God and Father of our Lord Jesus Christ, who has blessed us in the heavenly realms with every spiritual blessing in Christ.

EPHESIANS 1:3 NIV

"I will repay you for the years the locusts have eaten."

JOEL 2:25 NIV

His divine power has given us everything we need for a godly life through our knowledge of him who called us by his own glory and goodness.

2 PETER 1:3 NIV

A Heart of Gratitude

Jesus, cultivate within me a heart
of gratitude, for both the simple
things and the profound.
A smile, a teardrop, a gentle
rain. Reminders of Your presence
surround me, but sometimes I am
so focused on what I do not have,
that I forget how much I actually
possess. Thank You, thank You,
for Your lavish blessings. Amen.

Come, Thou Fount of every blessing,
Tune my heart to sing Thy grace;
Streams of mercy, never ceasing,
Call for songs of loudest praise.
Teach me some melodious sonnet,
Sung by flaming tongues above.
Praise the mount! I'm fixed upon it,
Mount of Thy redeeming love.

ROBERT ROBINSON

The unthankful heart discovers no
mercies; but the thankful heart will find,
in every hour, some heavenly blessings.

HENRY WARD BEECHER

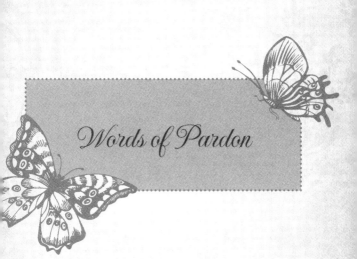

Words of Pardon

"Then neither do I condemn you,"
Jesus declared. "Go now and
leave your life of sin."
JOHN 8:11 NIV

The humiliation must have been unbearable. As if the scorning and judgmental faces of the townspeople weren't enough, the disdain from those who loved the woman caught in adultery would have made her crimson with shame. Would her family still claim her? Would her friends utter her name?

Everyone has a story, and no doubt the woman caught in adultery had hers. She had her reasons, more likely an act of desperation than wanton sin and debauchery. Perhaps it paid the bills, provided for her children, gave her a sense of power, or provided her with some sort of identity.

Whatever the reason, being dragged through town and before Jesus no doubt caused her to reconsider. Surely she expected nothing but condemnation from this mysterious man who quietly wrote in the dirt. Instead, she received a gift. The gift of pardon. Sweet relief. What an unexpected, but cherished blessing.

No matter *what* you've done, this gift is yours for the taking.

But he was pierced for our transgressions,
he was crushed for our iniquities;
the punishment that brought us peace was
on him, and by his wounds we are healed.

ISAIAH 53:5 NIV

"Whenever you stand praying, forgive,
if you have anything against anyone,
so that your Father who is in heaven will
also forgive you your transgressions."

MARK 11:25 NASB

Forgive Me

Heavenly Father, my sin is so ugly. I want to
hide. I feel ashamed for my actions. But,
like a refreshing wind on a sun-scalded day,
You forgive me. A breath of air, relief. I am so
grateful, I cannot find the words. Thank You
for cleansing me so completely from my sin.
Walk with me now as I turn away from it,
and live my life for You. Amen.

Have mercy on me, O God, because of your unfailing love. Because of your great compassion, blot out the stain of my sins. Wash me clean from my guilt. Purify me from my sin.
PSALM 51:1–2 NLT

Purify me from my sins, and I will be clean; wash me, and I will be whiter than snow.
PSALM 51:7 NLT

Forgiveness is an act of the will,
and the will can function regardless
of the temperature of the heart.

CORRIE TEN BOOM

Marvelous grace of our loving Lord,
grace that exceeds our sin and our guilt!
Yonder on Calvary's mount outpoured,
there where the blood of the Lamb was spilled.

JULIA H. JOHNSTON

What can wash away my sin?
Nothing but the blood of Jesus.

ROBERT LOWRY

"If my people, who are called by my name, will humble themselves and pray and seek my face and turn from their wicked ways, then will I hear from heaven, and I will forgive their sin and will heal their land."

2 Chronicles 7:14 NIV

Help us, O God of our salvation, for the glory of Your name; And deliver us and forgive our sins for Your name's sake.

Psalm 79:9 NASB

Teach Me to Forgive

Jesus, what a joy it is to be
forgiven, to know that You do
not hold my sins against me.
I am puzzled then, as to why it is
sometimes so difficult for me to
forgive others. I hold on to my
unforgiveness, cherishing it like
a prize, reluctant to release it to
Your grace-filled, nail-pierced
hands. Teach me to forgive,
as You have forgiven me. Amen.

*Who can discern their own errors? Forgive my
hidden faults. Keep your servant also
from willful sins; may they not rule
over me. Then I will be blameless,
innocent of great transgression.*

PSALM 19:12–13 NIV

*"Forgive us our debts, as we
also have forgiven our debtors."*

MATTHEW 6:12 NIV

*If we confess our sins, he is faithful and
just and will forgive us our sins and
purify us from all unrighteousness.*

1 JOHN 1:9 NIV

Forgiveness is the final form of love.

REINHOLD NIEBUHR

You can't undo anything you've already
done, but you can face up to it. You can tell
the truth. You can seek forgiveness.
And then let God do the rest.

UNKNOWN

"This is my blood of the covenant, which is poured
out for many for the forgiveness of sins."
MATTHEW 26:28 NIV

He is so rich in kindness and grace that
he purchased our freedom with the blood
of his Son and forgave our sins.
EPHESIANS 1:7 NLT

In fact, the law requires that nearly everything
be cleansed with blood, and without the
shedding of blood there is no forgiveness.
HEBREWS 9:22 NIV

Forgiving Myself

Father, You promise to cast my sins as far as the east is from the west. But I find it difficult to forgive myself. I hold myself to unattainable standards then despise myself for not keeping my rules. Am I saying that I am better than You? That You can forgive me, but I cannot? Help me to let go of my sin, once and for all. Amen.

Arise, my soul, arise; shake off thy guilty fears;
The bleeding sacrifice in my behalf appears:
Before the throne my surety stands,
My name is written on His hands.
CHARLES WESLEY

Forgiveness is the fragrance that the violet
sheds on the heel that has crushed it.
MARK TWAIN

Words of Promise

"*For he made this promise to our ancestors, to Abraham and his children forever.*"

LUKE 1:55 NLT

Can you imagine trying to grasp the news? Not only are you pregnant—a teenager no less—but you are also unmarried, a virgin. As if that isn't shocking enough, you happen to be carrying the promised Messiah in your womb. How could this possibly be so?

The first person Jesus touched on earth was His mother. Before He could even speak, the Word changed Mary, and she knew deep in her heart that this was an encounter like no other. Despite her shock, despite the havoc He wreaked in her life, Mary embraced her Father's promise and this new purpose for living with every fiber of her being. "Oh, how my soul praises the Lord. How my spirit rejoices in God my Savior!" (Luke 1:46–47 NLT).

Interestingly, throughout the Gospels, Jesus never uses the phrase, "I promise." Why? Because He is the promise. . .for Mary, for you, for a thousand generations. Take a moment right now to quiet your soul and praise Him for being the peace-bringing, life-changing, everlasting promise.

"Be strong and courageous. Do not be
afraid or terrified because of them,
for the LORD your God goes with you;
he will never leave you nor forsake you."
DEUTERONOMY 31:6 NIV

But immediately Jesus spoke to them, saying,
"Take courage, it is I; do not be afraid."
MATTHEW 14:27 NASB

The Promised One

Jesus, You are the promise, the One spoken of for generations, the One who cleanses us from our sins, brings us to the throne, and makes us righteous before the Father. How I rejoice in You—I am bursting with song. Thank You for life that brings so much promise. Amen.

*"Praise be to the LORD, who has given rest
to his people Israel just as he promised.
Not one word has failed of all the good promises
he gave through his servant Moses."*
1 KINGS 8:56 NIV

*"My prayer is not that you take them out of the
world but that you protect them from the evil one."*
JOHN 17:15 NIV

Let God's promises shine on your problems.

CORRIE TEN BOOM

An infinite God can give all of Himself
to each of His children. He does not
distribute Himself that each may have
a part, but to each one He gives all of
Himself as fully as if there were no others.

A. W. TOZER

"Look, the winter is past, and the rains are over
and gone. The flowers are springing up,
the season of singing birds has come,
and the cooing of turtledoves fills the air."

SONG OF SOLOMON 2:11–12 NLT

Dear brothers and sisters, when troubles come
your way, consider it an opportunity for great joy.
For you know that when your faith is tested,
your endurance has a chance to grow.

JAMES 1:2–3 NLT

Problems or Opportunities?

Father, when I see problems,
You see opportunities to reveal
Your love, to provide, to meet
my needs in ways that I could
never dream. Help me to see my
problems as opportunities to draw
closer to You, and to allow You to
solve them in Your creative love
and graciousness for me. Amen.

He made heaven and earth,
the sea, and everything in them.
He keeps every promise forever.

PSALM 146:6 NLT

Therefore, the promise comes by faith,
so that it may be by grace and may be
guaranteed to all Abraham's offspring—
not only to those who are of the law but
also to those who have the faith of Abraham.
He is the father of us all.

ROMANS 4:16 NIV

God has plans—
not problems—
for our lives.

CORRIE TEN BOOM

Darkness may o'ertake me and my song
forsake me, but alone I shall never be;
for the Friend beside me promised He would
guide me and will keep His promise to me.

JAMES ROWE

And this is God's plan: Both Gentiles and Jews who believe the Good News share equally in the riches inherited by God's children. Both are part of the same body, and both enjoy the promise of blessings because they belong to Christ Jesus.

EPHESIANS 3:6 NLT

Let us hold unswervingly to the hope we profess, for he who promised is faithful.

HEBREWS 10:23 NIV

Words of Peace

"I have told you these things, so that in
me you may have peace. In this world
you will have trouble. But take heart!
I have overcome the world."

JOHN 16:33 NIV

As the final days of Jesus' life drew near, the disciples must have been beside themselves with worry. They tried to understand what was about to happen, but could they really? It was so difficult to wrap their brains around all that Jesus was saying. They were confused, overwhelmed, overcome with fear about the future. And Jesus didn't shy away from the truth—things were about to get tough—almost unbearably so. But, just when all hope seemed to be lost, He promised them peace. Can you hear His gentle voice, the words trickling down the disciples' hearts, settling deep into their souls? "Yes, you will have trouble," Jesus said, "but you will also have peace! I have already overcome, there's nothing to fear."

The peace of Jesus is difficult, if not impossible to explain, but it is yours for the taking. May His peace reside deep within your soul.

*But I will sing of your strength, in the morning
I will sing of your love; for you are my fortress,
my refuge in times of trouble.*
PSALM 59:16 NIV

*Instead, I have calmed and quieted myself,
like a weaned child who no longer cries for its mother's
milk. Yes, like a weaned child is my soul within me.*
PSALM 131:2 NLT

Those who have the wind of the Holy Spirit
in their souls glide ahead even while they
sleep. If the vessel of our soul is still being
tossed by winds or storms, we should wake the
Lord who has been resting with us all along,
and He will swiftly calm the sea.

BROTHER LAWRENCE

Pray and let God worry.

MARTIN LUTHER

Never be afraid to trust an
unknown future to a known God.

CORRIE TEN BOOM

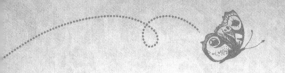

"I will see you again and you will rejoice,
and no one will take away your joy."
JOHN 16:22 NIV

"See, God has come to save me. I will trust in him
and not be afraid. The LORD GOD is my strength
and my song; he has given me victory."
ISAIAH 12:2 NLT

I myself will tend my sheep and give them a place
to lie down in peace, says the Sovereign LORD.
EZEKIEL 34:15 NLT

Settle Me Down

Jesus, in a world of trouble and confusion,
I need Your peace. As my problems surround
me and threaten to overtake me, Your peace
settles me down. Remind me of it when my
mind wanders, as it is so likely to do.
Thank You for the gift of peace. Amen.

The LORD gives strength to his people;
the LORD blesses his people with peace.

PSALM 29:11 NIV

Do not be anxious about anything,
but in every situation, by prayer and petition,
with thanksgiving, present your requests to God.
And the peace of God, which transcends all
understanding, will guard your hearts
and your minds in Christ Jesus.

PHILIPPIANS 4:6–7 NIV

Blessed are the single-hearted, for they shall enjoy much peace. If you refuse to be hurried and pressed, if you stay your soul on God, nothing can keep you from that clearness of spirit which is life and peace. In that stillness you will know what His will is.

AMY CARMICHAEL

Our anxiety does not empty tomorrow of its sorrow, but only empties today of its strength.

CHARLES SPURGEON

Solitude is the furnace of transformation.

HENRI NOUWEN

Therefore, since we have been justified through faith, we have peace with God through our Lord Jesus Christ.

ROMANS 5:1 NIV

"I will make a covenant of peace with them; it will be an everlasting covenant. I will establish them and increase their numbers, and I will put my sanctuary among them forever."

EZEKIEL 37:26 NIV

Finally, Peace

Jesus, before You died, we were separated from God. There was no peace—sin was the ugly barrier that stood in the way. Thank You for Your death that brought peace. Thank You that I can now draw near to my heavenly Father, with nothing to stand in the way. Amen.

*"Glory to God in the highest heaven, and on earth
peace to those on whom his favor rests."*
LUKE 2:14 NIV

*May the God of hope fill you with all joy and peace
as you trust in him, so that you may overflow with
hope by the power of the Holy Spirit.*
ROMANS 15:13 NIV

*But the fruit of the Spirit is love, joy, peace,
forbearance, kindness, goodness, faithfulness.*
GALATIANS 5:22 NIV

Our hearts are restless until
they find their rest in Thee.
SAINT AUGUSTINE

Peace, peace, sweet peace, wonderful gift
from above, Oh wonderful wonderful peace,
sweet peace, the gift of God's love.
PETER P. BILHORN

And let the peace that comes from Christ rule in your hearts. For as members of one body you are called to live in peace. And always be thankful.
COLOSSIANS 3:15 NLT

Now may the God of peace make you holy in every way, and may your whole spirit and soul and body be kept blameless until our Lord Jesus Christ comes again.
1 THESSALONIANS 5:23 NLT

Words of
Sanctification

"But the Advocate, the Holy Spirit. . .
will teach you all things and will remind
you of everything I have said to you."

JOHN 14:26 NIV

For three years, Jesus was with them, teaching, modeling, leading. The disciples were both confused and amazed by this man who taught them how to live. Now He was leaving. Repeatedly He said to be like Him, but without Him near, how would they do this? How would they remember? How would they carry on His ministry without His presence?

In place of His physical presence, Jesus left the disciples—and us—the marvelous gift of the Holy Spirit. Through the power of the Spirit, the disciples would be made more like their beloved Master. Over time, they would be molded and shaped into the men He created them to be. Sanctification. This process begins with the truth of God, opening our eyes to our former way of life, then offers what Jesus did—an entirely new perspective on ancient truths established at the beginning of time. The Holy Spirit is the gift that keeps on giving, providing the daily guidance, the conviction, and the gentle nudging that guides us on a Christlike path.

"Sanctify them in the truth;
Your word is truth."

John 17:17 NASB

"If you love me, keep my commands. And I will ask
the Father, and he will give you another advocate
to help you and be with you forever—the Spirit
of truth. The world cannot accept him, because it
neither sees him nor knows him. But you know
him, for he lives with you and will be in you."

John 14:15–17 NIV

To deny oneself is to be aware only of
Christ and no more of self, to see only
Him who goes before and no more on
the road which is too hard for us.

DIETRICH BONHOEFFER

Nobody ever outgrows scripture;
the Book widens and deepens with our years.

CHARLES H. SPURGEON

Happiness can be found neither in ourselves
or in external things, but in God and
in ourselves as united to Him.

PASCAL

But now you are free from the power
of sin and have become slaves of God.
Now you do those things that lead to
holiness and result in eternal life.

ROMANS 6:22 NLT

"Keep all my decrees by putting them into practice,
for I am the LORD who makes you holy."

LEVITICUS 20:8 NLT

More Like You

Father, I long to be made holy,
and to be molded into the
likeness of Your Son. I want to
see the world through His eyes,
and not my own. Help me to be
cooperative with the process of
sanctification so that I am made
more like You. Amen.

"Abide in Me, and I in you. As the branch cannot bear fruit of itself unless it abides in the vine, so neither can you unless you abide in Me. I am the vine, you are the branches; he who abides in Me and I in him, he bears much fruit, for apart from Me you can do nothing."

JOHN 15:4–5 NASB

Whatever weakens your reason, impairs the tenderness of your conscience, obscures your sense of God, takes off your relish for spiritual things, whatever increases the authority of the body over the mind, that thing is sin to you, however innocent it may seem in itself.

SUSANNA WESLEY

Thirsty hearts are those whose longings
have been wakened by the touch
of God within them.

A. W. TOZER

We have been made holy through the sacrifice
of the body of Jesus Christ once for all.
HEBREWS 10:10 NIV

It is God's will that you
should be sanctified.
1 THESSALONIANS 4:3 NIV

But now that you have been set free from sin and
have become slaves of God, the benefit you reap
leads to holiness, and the result is eternal life.
ROMANS 6:22 NIV

Abiding in You

Jesus, the secret to being sanctified is remaining in You. So why am I so tempted to step outside Your loving arms? Teach me what it means to abide in You, to allow my thoughts, my words, my actions to flow through the filter of Your grace. Make me more like You. Amen.

So also Jesus suffered and died outside
the city gates to make his people
holy by means of his own blood.
HEBREWS 13:12 NLT

It is because of him that you are in Christ Jesus,
who has become for us wisdom from God—
that is, our righteousness, holiness and redemption.
1 CORINTHIANS 1:30 NIV

Words of Compassion

When the Lord saw her,
his heart overflowed with
compassion. "Don't cry!" he said.

LUKE 7:13 NLT

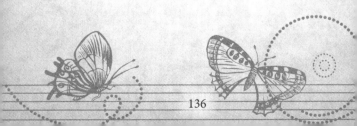

Not only had she lost her only son, she was a widow, never more alone in her entire life. The grief must have been unbearable, as her friends held her up, willing her to move, to attend to her son's burial. When Jesus came upon the scene, His heart broke. He certainly wasn't obligated to bring the widow's son back to life, but He acted out of a heart filled with compassion. How He longed to hold her, to tell her that this life is temporary. If only He could soothe her wounds for just a moment. So He gave her the one thing He knew would heal her breaking heart—He gave her back her son.

Jesus' heart of compassion moved Him to heal the sick, to raise the dead, to give sight to the blind and music to those who could not hear. Jesus' compassion enabled Him to serve others in ways that changed them completely.

How can your heart of compassion move you to touch others with His love?

Seeing the people, He felt compassion for them,
because they were distressed and dispirited
like sheep without a shepherd.
MATTHEW 9:36 NASB

✦

When Jesus saw her weeping. . .he was deeply
moved in spirit and troubled. . . . Jesus wept.
JOHN 11:33–35 NIV

✦

But you, Lord, are a compassionate
and gracious God, slow to anger,
abounding in love and faithfulness.
PSALM 86:15 NIV

You may call God love, you may call
God goodness. But the best name
for God is compassion.

MEISTER ECKHART

Love divine, all loves excelling,
Joy of heaven to earth come down;
Fix in us thy humble dwelling;
All thy faithful mercies crown!
Jesus, Thou art all compassion,
Pure unbounded love Thou art;
Visit us with Thy salvation;
Enter every trembling heart.

CHARLES WESLEY

As a father has compassion on his children,
so the LORD has compassion on those who fear him.

PSALM 103:13 NIV

Jesus saw the huge crowd as he stepped
from the boat, and he had compassion
on them and healed their sick.

MATTHEW 14:14 NLT

You will again have compassion on us;
you will tread our sins underfoot and hurl
all our iniquities into the depths of the sea.

MICAH 7:19 NIV

A Healing Balm

Father, I am surrounded by empty, aching
people. It is tempting to numb myself to their
pain, to look the other way so that I don't
have to act. But this is not what You desire.
Soften my heart. Fill it with compassion,
just like Jesus, so that I may touch others with
the healing balm of Your love. Amen.

The Lord is good to all;
he has compassion on all he has made.

PSALM 145:9 NIV

"For a brief moment I abandoned you,
but with great compassion I will take you
back. In a burst of anger I turned my
face away for a little while. But with
everlasting love I will have compassion
on you," says the Lord, your Redeemer.

ISAIAH 54:7–8 NLT

It is a great consolation for me to remember
that the Lord, to whom I had drawn near
in humble and childlike faith, has suffered
and died for me, and that He will look
on me in love and compassion.

WOLFGANG AMADEUS MOZART

Man may dismiss compassion
from his heart, but God never will.

WILLIAM COWPER

*For he says to Moses, "I will have mercy
on whom I have mercy, and I will have
compassion on whom I have compassion."*

ROMANS 9:15 NIV

*Shout for joy, you heavens; rejoice,
you earth; burst into song, you mountains!
For the LORD comforts his people and will
have compassion on his afflicted ones.*

ISAIAH 49:13 NIV

The Gift of Comfort

Thank You, Father, for the gift of
comfort. Even though the world
brings trouble, You bring comfort
to my aching, anxious heart.
Thank You for this gift that
soothes me despite my difficult
circumstances. Thank You that I can
share this gift with others. Amen.

*Praise be to the God and Father
of our Lord Jesus Christ, the Father
of compassion and the God of all
comfort, who comforts us in all our
troubles, so that we can comfort those
in any trouble with the comfort we
ourselves receive from God.*

2 CORINTHIANS 1:3–4 NIV

The Gospel Call

Jesus replied, "Anyone who drinks this water will soon become thirsty again. But those who drink the water I give will never be thirsty again. It becomes a fresh, bubbling spring within them, giving them eternal life."

JOHN 4:13–14 NLT

She was no doubt thirsty, perhaps literally, but she knew, and He knew. The relief she sought would not be found at the bottom of a well. There was an emptiness in her soul, an ache that could not be soothed. But she tried. She numbed her pain in the arms of one man after another, divorcing them, finally giving up marriage entirely. She would just get thirsty again.

Then she encountered the One of her dreams. Of course she didn't know it at first. But this wise man, who knew everything about her, was the One she'd been longing for, whose arms would never tire of her, who would never discard her. He would hold her for eternity. She would never thirst again. "Could it be?" she asked, her heart afraid to believe it was true. "Could this man *really* be the Messiah?"

The woman at the well responded to the call of the Gospel, and then she did what we can do: she ran and told everyone the marvelous news.

Jesus told them, "This is the only work God wants from you: Believe in the one he has sent."
JOHN 6:29 NLT

"For the Son of Man came to seek and save those who are lost."
LUKE 19:10 NLT

I cannot make myself right with God, I cannot make my life perfect; I can only be right with God if I accept the atonement of the Lord Jesus Christ as an absolute gift.

OSWALD CHAMBERS

All who call on God in true faith, earnestly from the heart, will certainly be heard.

MARTIN LUTHER

Jesus does not give recipes that show the way to God as other teachers of religion do. He Himself is the way.

KARL BARTH

"Yes, I am the gate. Those who come in through me will be saved. They will come and go freely and will find good pastures."

JOHN 10:9 NLT

Peter replied, "Repent and be baptized, every one of you, in the name of Jesus Christ for the forgiveness of your sins. And you will receive the gift of the Holy Spirit."

ACTS 2:38 NIV

In my desperation I prayed, and the LORD listened; he saved me from all my troubles.

PSALM 34:6 NLT

The Good News

Jesus, thank You for the Good News of
the Gospel. Thank You for its simplicity,
its relevance, and for the joy it brings.
Teach me to share it with others in a way that is
honest, meaningful, and true. Help me to burst
with it, a secret too good not to share. Amen.

*God our Savior. . .wants all. . .to be saved
and to come to a knowledge of the truth.*
1 TIMOTHY 2:3–4 NIV

*Jesus said to her, "I am the resurrection and
the life. The one who believes in me will live,
even though they die; and whoever lives by believing
in me will never die. Do you believe this?"*
JOHN 11:25–26 NIV

There is a God-shaped vacuum in the heart
of every man which cannot be filled by any
created thing, but only by God, the Creator,
made known through Jesus.

BLAISE PASCAL

Crown Him the Lord of life,
who triumphed over the grave,
And rose victorious in the strife
for those He came to save.
His glories now we sing,
who died, and rose on high,
Who died eternal life to bring,
and lives that death may die.

MATTHEW BRIDGES

And this is the way to have eternal life—
to know you, the only true God,
and Jesus Christ, the one you sent to earth.
JOHN 17:3 NLT

And Jesus said to the woman,
"Your faith has saved you; go in peace."
LUKE 7:50 NLT

And since we have been made right in God's
sight by the blood of Christ, he will certainly
save us from God's condemnation.
ROMANS 5:9 NLT

White as Snow

Merciful Father, I praise You. Thank You for
saving me, for washing me white as snow,
and for the gift of the Holy Spirit, poured over
me through Christ. Thank You for Your grace
and the promise and hope of eternal life. Amen.

*He saved us, not because of righteous things we
had done, but because of his mercy. He saved us
through the washing of rebirth and renewal by the
Holy Spirit, whom he poured out on us generously
through Jesus Christ our Savior, so that,
having been justified by his grace, we might become
heirs having the hope of eternal life.*
TITUS 3:5–7 NIV

Words of Wisdom

"The Son of Man came eating and drinking, and they say, 'Here is a glutton and a drunkard, a friend of tax collectors and sinners.' But wisdom is proved right by her deeds."

MATTHEW 11:19 NIV

There is a difference between knowledge and wisdom. Knowledge is attained. Wisdom is acquired. Knowledge is about amassing facts and details. Wisdom knows the facts, but is more concerned about the big picture, knowing when to apply the facts to the appropriate context.

Jesus constantly challenged His listeners to see the big picture. To consider the knowledge they'd gained in a completely different light, to learn to apply it appropriately, to understand the spirit, not just the letter of the law.

For us, this doesn't happen overnight, nor does it come naturally. Wisdom is acquired by years of practice, learning from others, opening hearts and minds to the teaching of Jesus, and learning to apply it appropriately through the guidance of the Holy Spirit.

The LORD says, "I will guide you
along the best pathway for your life.
I will advise you and watch over you.
PSALM 32:8 NLT

Jesus said, "For judgment I have come into
this world, so that the blind will see and
those who see will become blind."
JOHN 9:39 NIV

And Jesus grew in wisdom and stature,
and in favor with God and man.
LUKE 2:52 NIV

I have held many things in my hands,
and I have lost them all; but whatever I have
placed in God's hands, that I still possess.

MARTIN LUTHER

Wisdom is the right use of knowledge.
To know is not to be wise. Many men know
a great deal, and are all the greater fools
for it. There is no fool so great a fool as
a knowing fool. But to know how to use
knowledge is to have wisdom.

CHARLES H. SPURGEON

"Anyone who listens to my teaching
and follows it is wise, like a person who
builds a house on solid rock. Though the
rain comes in torrents and the floodwaters
rise and the winds beat against that house,
it won't collapse because it is built on bedrock."

MATTHEW 7:24–25 NLT

"For the earth will be filled with
the knowledge of the glory of the
LORD, as the waters cover the sea."

HABAKKUK 2:14 NIV

My Finite Mind

Infinite Father, my mind is so finite.
My thoughts make so much sense to me, until
I examine them in the light of Your wisdom.
Help me to grow in my understanding of
You, and to invest my life in growing in
Your wisdom. Amen.

*"For my thoughts are not your thoughts,
neither are your ways my ways," declares the
LORD. "As the heavens are higher than the earth,
so are my ways higher than your ways and
my thoughts than your thoughts."*

ISAIAH 55:8–9 NIV

*In him lie hidden all the treasures
of wisdom and knowledge.*

COLOSSIANS 2:3 NLT

God, grant me the serenity to accept
the things I cannot change, the courage
to change the things I can, and the
wisdom to know the difference.

REINHOLD NIEBUHR

When you read God's Word,
you must constantly be saying to yourself,
"It is talking to me, and about me."

SOREN KIERKEGAARD

"Getting wisdom is the wisest thing you can do!
And whatever else you do, develop good judgment."
PROVERBS 4:7 NLT

In all wisdom and insight He made known to us
the mystery of His will, according to His kind
intention which He purposed in Him.
EPHESIANS 1:8–9 NASB

"His wisdom is profound,
his power is vast."
JOB 9:4 NIV

Good Judgment

Jesus, I know all too well that my gut instinct is not always necessarily the best. I want to get wisdom! I long to be wise. I pray that Your Spirit would teach me about developing good judgment, that I would make decisions based on Your work in me and not what my gut tells me to do. Amen.

All this also comes from the LORD
Almighty, whose plan is wonderful,
whose wisdom is magnificent.

ISAIAH 28:29 NIV

I instruct you in the way of wisdom
and lead you along straight paths.

PROVERBS 4:11 NIV

Words of Light

When Jesus spoke again to the people,
he said, "I am the light of the world.
Whoever follows me will never walk in
darkness, but will have the light of life."

JOHN 8:12 NIV

The Good News is portrayed beautifully in John 8:12. Jesus is the Light, and He promises the light of life to all who follow Him. Jesus possessed two qualities that enabled Him to share this message without wavering. The first was complete confidence in His identity and His purpose. He was the Light, the Son of God, whether others acknowledged Him or not, and His purpose was clear: To do the will of the One who sent Him (John 6:38). Additionally, He had no interest in being a people pleaser, nor did He have a need to tell them what they wanted to hear. His unswerving commitment was to His Father, and this was the driving force behind every word He spoke. The Good News of the Gospel naturally flowed out of this commitment.

The natural response to receiving the light is to share it with others. When you are completely confident in your identity in Christ, your life purpose becomes clear and you are free from the temptation to be a people pleaser. This dark world is desperate for the Light.

For with you is the fountain of life;
in your light we see light.

Then God said, "Let there be light," and there
was light. And God saw that the light was good.
Then he separated the light from the darkness.

When you look at the inner workings of electrical things, you see wires. Until the current passes through them, there will be no light. That wire is you and me. The current is God. We have the power to let the current pass through us, use us, to produce the Light of the world, Jesus, in us. Or we can refuse to be used and allow darkness to spread.

MOTHER TERESA

*"Believe in the light while you have the light,
so that you may become children of light."*
JOHN 12:36 NIV

*"The eye is the lamp of the body. If your eyes are
healthy, your whole body will be full of light."*
MATTHEW 6:22 NIV

*"Put your trust in the light
while there is still time."*
JOHN 12:36 NLT

Fill Me with Your Light

Jesus, I want to be filled with Your light. This dark world is aching for light, for good news, for a Savior. You have done so much for me, I just have to share it with others. Fill me with Your light, and help me be a beacon to all I encounter. Amen.

For once you were full of darkness, but now you
have light from the Lord. So live as people of light!
EPHESIANS 5:8 NLT

For with you is the fountain of life;
in your light we see light.
PSALM 36:9 NIV

"Arise, shine, for your light has come,
and the glory of the LORD rises upon you."
ISAIAH 60:1 NIV

We stumble and fall constantly even
when we are most enlightened.
But when we are in true spiritual darkness,
we do not even know that we have fallen.

THOMAS MERTON

Turn your eyes upon Jesus,
Look full in His wonderful face,
And the things of earth
will grow strangely dim,
In the light of His glory and grace.

HELEN H. LEMMEL

Come, descendants of Jacob,
let us walk in the light of the LORD.
ISAIAH 2:5 NIV

But everything exposed by the light
becomes visible—and everything that
is illuminated becomes a light.
EPHESIANS 5:13 NIV

You are dressed in a robe of light.
You stretch out the starry curtain of the heavens.
PSALM 104:2 NLT

Shine Your Light

Father, without Your light shining on my path,
the way looks dark and dreary. I am filled
with fear. I am amazed how differently things
appear when Your light shines and brightens
my journey. Thank You that I no longer have
to walk in darkness. Amen.

For God, who said, "Let there be light in the darkness," has made this light shine in our hearts so we could know the glory of God that is seen in the face of Jesus Christ.

2 CORINTHIANS 4:6 NLT

This is the message we heard from Jesus and now declare to you: God is light, and there is no darkness in him at all.

1 JOHN 1:5 NLT

The Hope of Heaven

"My Father's house has many rooms;
if that were not so, would I have told you that
I am going there to prepare a place for you?
And if I go and prepare a place for you,
I will come back and take you to be with me
that you also may be where I am."

JOHN 14:2–3 NIV

It is their last night together. The atmosphere is charged with electricity, mystery. The words Jesus speaks this night are all at once terrifying and exhilarating. There is fear, there is peace. Then a promise: I am going to prepare a place for you. I will come for you and take you where I am.

The One who was at the creation of the world has now promised to create a new home for His loved ones. Can you imagine, as you gaze upon the beauty and majesty of earthly creation, what heaven must be like? If the Creator invested so much time and detail in the glory of the Grand Canyon, the intricacies of a hummingbird, how much more marvelous must heaven be? It is beyond our mind's ability to comprehend.

But we have the promise, spoken by the Word. He prepares a place for us and we will be with Him for Life. Everlasting, eternal, glorious life.

"Repent, for the kingdom
of heaven has come near."
MATTHEW 3:2 NIV

◎

Yet God has made everything beautiful
for its own time. He has planted eternity
in the human heart, but even so,
people cannot see the whole scope of
God's work from beginning to end.
ECCLESIASTES 3:11 NLT

◎

And in this fellowship we enjoy
the eternal life he promised us.
1 JOHN 2:25 NLT

My Inheritance

My Father in heaven, I have an inheritance!
In a world where thieves and moths and
rust destroy, when seemingly precious
things are so cheap and temporary, I am
thrilled beyond measure at the thought of an
inheritance reserved for me. Thank You
for this marvelous promise. Amen.

*Praise be to the God and Father of our Lord Jesus
Christ! In his great mercy he has given us new
birth into a living hope through the resurrection
of Jesus Christ from the dead, and into an
inheritance that can never perish, spoil or fade.
This inheritance is kept in heaven for you.*

1 PETER 1:3–4 NIV

I've read the last page of the Bible.
It's all going to turn out all right.
BILLY GRAHAM

Oh how swiftly the glory
of the world passes away!
THOMAS À KEMPIS

The door on which we have been
knocking all our lives will open at last.
C. S. LEWIS

" 'He will wipe every tear from their eyes.
There will be no more death' or mourning or crying
or pain, for the old order of things has passed away."
REVELATION 21:4 NIV

Then God will give you a grand entrance
into the eternal Kingdom of our
Lord and Savior Jesus Christ.
2 PETER 1:11 NLT

Forever with Him

Jesus, You are the Word, the Light
of the world. Thank You for Your
wonderful words and all the life
they offer me. I long for the day
when the trumpet will sound
and I will meet You in the air.
I cannot wait to be with
You forever. Amen.

*For the Lord himself will come down from heaven,
with a loud command, with the voice of the
archangel and with the trumpet call of God,
and the dead in Christ will rise first. After that,
we who are still alive and are left will be caught up
together with them in the clouds to meet the Lord
in the air. And so we will be with the Lord forever.*

1 Thessalonians 4:16–17 NIV